HIGH FIVES
ARE BETTER THAN
FACEPALMS

A QUICK GUIDE TO GETTING YOUR LIFE TOGETHER

C. S. JOHNSON

Copyright © 2025 by C. S. Johnson.

All rights reserved. This book or any portion thereof may not be reproduced or used in any manner whatsoever without the express written permission of the publisher. For any questions, comments, or concerns, please email me or contact me through my website at www.csjohnson.me.

ISBN ebook: 978-1-948464-96-3
ISBN Hardback: 978-1-948464-97-0

Back cover art by L. S. Johnson. Copyright paid for by C. S. Johnson.

DEDICATION

To my friends and family members who see a lot of my bad days. You see a lot of the ugly so I can glean a little beauty out of the goodness, and I am so grateful for your sacrifice; I truly can never repay you for all the goodness, truth, beauty, and love you have given me.

I wrote this book because a lot of you asked me how I put it all together and keep it that way. Life isn't always perfect, but I am so glad that even when everything is upset and things seem beyond control, I have a God who loves me and friends and family who can help me pick up all the pieces and start again. Thank you for being an inspiration to me and my readers!

C. S. JOHNSON

INTRODUCTION
High Fives are Better than Facepalms

Life is Hard

Anyone who says life is easy is delusional at best, and a deceiver at worst.

And I don't know about you, but I don't like it when people lie to me, and I especially don't like it when their lies waste my time. And since I don't even like it when people who *don't* lie to me waste my time, I'm going to get through this introduction part quick.

After all, it's in the title: *High Fives are Better Than Facepalms: A **Quick** Guide to Getting Your Life Together.*

And if I've learned nothing else in all my years of being a writer and writing books, it's that book titles should not be too terribly misleading.

You wanted quick, so you ought to get it.

So here we go …

Life is hard.

It's not something that's explicitly stated enough. In some ways, I blame technology for this. We are insulated from some of the harsher realities of life because of progress and especially technological use. It's easy to think life is easy when you're only a few presses of a button away from getting tacos delivered to your house.

Recently, I rewatched *The Jetsons* with my kids, and I laughed at how George Jetson's biggest problem at work is getting his fingers hurt from pushing buttons all day. I laughed because the man had a point, and it's even funnier to realize they'd thought of that all the way back in the 1950s.

The Jetsons becoming a satire was one of the more surprising aspects of growing up I have appreciated.

Since I've grown up and gotten some education and life experience, I can see more clearly than ever that life is hard. When I was young, I didn't think about all the work—all the time, sacrifice, blood, sweat, and tears—that went into even the smallest things. I took for granted that I would have a family, a house, a good school, and a bright future, even if others weren't so "lucky."

It's taken me a long time to see that luck has an extremely limited role in how life turns out, and even longer to see everyone truly is facing some kind of hard challenge in their lives. Especially now that I have kids, and life gets increasingly more complicated and confusing at times, I know how important it is to manage things.

I wrote this book to help you get your life more organized, too.

It might surprise you to know I'm actually pretty lazy at times, and it's hard to motivate me, but I consider organizing my life a matter of efficiency, and since the one consistent motivator I have in life is to help people, I wanted to write this.

I like helping people. These are life lessons I've learned, and I think of them as a gift I can pass onto you, in a very "hands to heart" kind of way.

This is the big one I want to start with here:

Pay attention to yourself, and how you respond to your life.

We are agents of change as well as recipients of it. How you respond to your life will affect how others respond to theirs, too.

Getting your life in order may help others do the same, and the more organized something is, the less likely more problems will arise from it. As the old-school teachers say, "A problem well-stated is a problem half-solved."

And we could all benefit from less problems in our lives.

Understanding how you will react and how you need to grow as an individual—as well as how you need to grow as a friend, family, or community—is critical for having a life that not only means something to you, but one that you can understand, and how it extends beyond you into your community.

One of Sun Tzu's proverbs from *The Art of War* speaks on how necessary this skill is:

> *"If you know the enemy and know yourself, you need not fear the result of a hundred battles. If you know yourself but not the enemy, for every victory gained, you will suffer a defeat. If you know neither the enemy nor yourself, you will succumb in every battle."*

So this is good news for all the narcissists out there: The first step to getting your life together is knowing yourself. The bad news for all the narcissists out there is you're going to have to be honest with yourself about it. And I mean you must be actually honest: Not overly critical, not overly merciful, not offering justifications for every perceived flaw—just honest.

I'm not eager to sit here and recommend a bunch of personality quizzes. If I had to recommend a few, it would be only because I know there are some truly terrible ones out there.

The Meyers-Briggs, the OCEAN Personality Test, and the DISC Assessment are the only ones I would agree are still good to use. For Christians out there, because I am a proud-but-not-(too)-haughty, solid Bible-thumping church lady, I recommend reading Max Lucado's book *Cure for the Common Life* where he further talks about this in context of spiritual gifts and callings.

All of this matters because the same thing is true, no matter where you are or what you believe: We have to know where we are if we want to know where we are going.

And while we may not agree with what constitutes a "good life," or a "winning life," we all want to feel like we've won at life in the end.

We all want to cross the finish line and get a "high five"—a moment of pure, celebratory ecstasy.

And we especially want that more than we want to "facepalm" ourselves. Who wants a face-slap of immeasurable regret and self-disgust, especially at our stupid mistakes or moments of unexpected, existential crisis?

That is the simple gimmick of this book:

High Fives are Better than Facepalms.

And while we all can appreciate the well-timed meme of Jean-Luc Picard slamming his palm across his pate in aggravated, composed fury, I'm sure you want to live in a way where you can give yourself a high five at the end of each day, and you would then especially prefer a high five to a facepalm.

I know I do.

This is my own simplified system of order, and I've found that while it's simple, it's not always easy, but it's still helped me a lot. And I hope it will help you, too.

In the following chapters, which will not be long, I'm going to go through five areas I've found are best to get focused on, offer you some tips to get on a better track, and likely share some fun things about me and my heart I can't organically incorporate into my fiction.

So, you've been warned.

And with that, if you're brave enough—because I'm not sure if anyone is ever truly "ready"—let's go onto the first chapter.

But before you go, take a moment to give yourself a high five—you're already one step closer to getting your life more organized.

I'm cheering for you, every step of the way.

All the best,

C. S. Johnson

QUICK SUMMARY:

- ☐ Life is hard, and pretending otherwise is a waste of time.

- ☐ Getting your life together starts with being honest—starting with yourself.

- ☐ Organizing your life not only helps you—it helps those around you.

- ☐ Use your hand as a model to help keep track of your life, using one finger for each area of focus.

- ☐ Your ultimate goal is to get more high fives and fewer facepalms!

HIGH FIVES
ARE BETTER THAN
FACEPALMS

C. S. JOHNSON

CHAPTER ONE
Give Yourself a Hand

Life is Crazy

Life is crazy, but you don't have to be—and more importantly, you *shouldn't* want to be crazy.

Ever since I can remember, there's been a rush of marketing aimed at that kind of immature, prolonged-adolescent age group, telling you to "embrace your crazy" and "just do it" and "be true to yourself," but the people telling you that are the people that benefit from your inability to regulate yourself and your desires. The whole "Life is crazy, but you don't have to be—but it helps" movement is built on a satanic lie, straight from the pit of Hell.

If B.J. Novak's Ryan Howard is the one saying this in *The Office*, then you ought to know it's probably really terrible advice.

But you can also see that it's terrible advice in real-time. It is a well-known biblical proverb in Galatians 6:7 that states, "Do not be deceived: God is not mocked, for whatever one sows, that will he also reap."

You reap what you sow, and too many people today have sown crazy and reaped the whirlwind of crazy.

In today's vernacular, it's also the basis for the FAFO internet meme.

You don't have to be on the internet long to see self-control is perilously underrated in society today.

And because self-control is at the heart of our actions—or reactions, if you *don't* have self-control—I like to use the image of a hand.

Because just look at your hands!

They may not be "George Constanza hand-model" material, but they are truly full of beauty–and they can make so many more beautiful things, too.

Hands are part of so much of what we do.

We shake hands, hold hands, hold onto other people using our hands; we can offer comfort and love and friendship through side-hugs, shoulder touches, and more.

The Shakers, a heretical branch of the Quakers—something I know more than average about as a Pennsylvania native—had a great motto to illustrate this:

> ***"Hands to Work,***
> ***Hearts to God."***

We can also do terrible things with them. We can hit and punch and scratch and grab; we can fight and hurt and light matches, all with our hands and fingers.

There's a scene in the 2006 movie *Ultraviolent* where Milla Jovovich's character, Vi (Violet) talks to the child she is protecting, telling him about her relationships. She goes through her fingers to illustrate them:

" 'Comrade' [pinky finger], 'lover' [ring finger], 'wife' [middle finger], and this one [pointing to her index finger]... This one was going to say 'mother,' but then I got sick, and all that became impossible."

While I think she got the order wrong (as you should be married before you're a lover—believe me this is way less messy, and also how God intended it to be), I liked the idea of using fingers to represent relationships, and since I'm pretty sure I haven't watched this movie since it came out in 2006, it has clearly stuck with me.

These are the setups I think of instead:

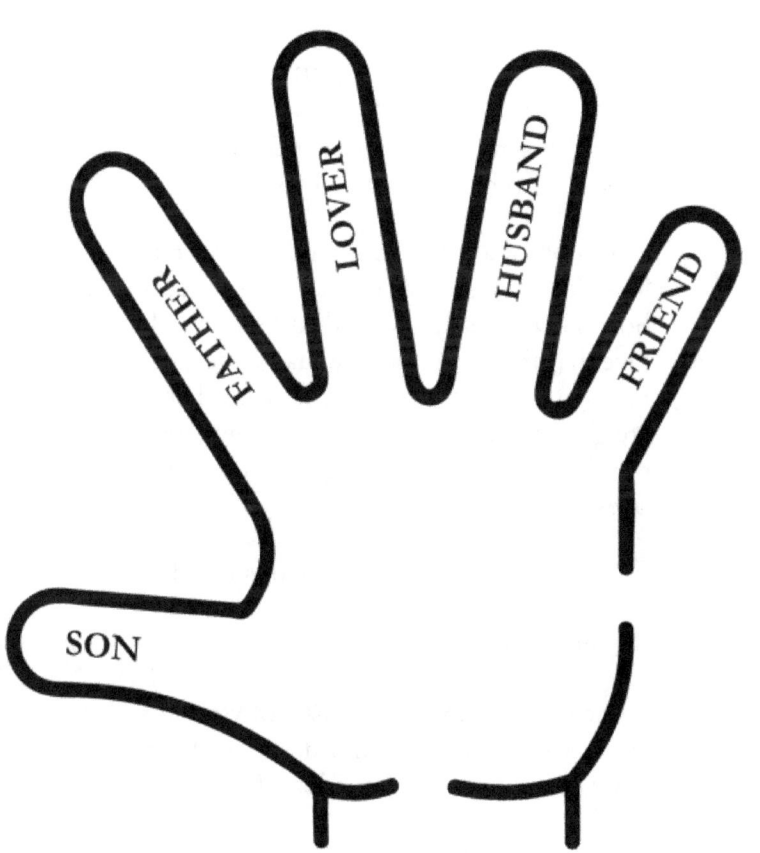

In the palm, you would write your name.

After all, humans are both individual and communal creatures—all of who you are is yourself, and it extends out to others in your chosen commitments and community.

Ultraviolet helped inspire this setup, as did *The Bonesetter's Daughter* (a 2001 book from Amy Tan I read in 2008). I loved that the main character, Ruth, uses her fingers and toes to keep her to-do list organized.

As a bit of a sidenote, as an author, I really love how strange my book DNA is, but also how much it really shows who I am, too. I love that this kind of thread has woven through my life to show me how our hands are great for cutting the madness out from our lives—and not just to give us the high fives or facepalms we earn.

When it comes to our lives, this is the breakdown of how our hands will help us organize our lives.

Each finger represents a part of your life you'll need to work on in order to gain the glory of your own majestic high five.

Let's go through them all, one by one:

HIGH FIVES
ARE BETTER THAN
FACEPALMS

Your life can be divided into five big categories, and I'm pleased to say they're all categories that begin with an "F."

FAITH

What do you believe about your life, and how do you fit into that belief?

What you believe matters, and it's the foundation of all that you do.

Even if you are not religious—and I highly recommend following Jesus anyway—you need to know what you believe, why you believe it, and how it will affect you in your life choices.

FAMILY & FRIENDS

Who do you care for? Who are the people that help take care of you, and who are the people you want to help succeed?

When we love someone, we want to work and sacrifice for their betterment. This means giving them our time, attention, and resources; more practically, it might mean calling your mom, emailing your friend you haven't talked to in a while, or visiting someone who's been there for you during times of change in your life.

FINANCES

What do you invest in? What do you value?

Your money is a symbol of who you are—how you earn it and where you spend it will tell anyone what you truly value.

Keeping it organized can be complicated, but there's no reason it can't be rewarding, too.

FITNESS

It's not always a matter of hitting the gym or skipping over dessert; keeping your mind from endlessly consuming slop, dibble, and plain content is also a way for you to respect yourself and show that you value yourself.

Your body is your outward shell—the layers of onion, if you Shrek fans will—that houses your soul here in this life. How you take care of it shows others you are responsible with what you've been given, and how well you do can also show how you can take care of others.

FUN

Finally, the easy part—or is it?

Yes, it is.

But what you do for fun can help you find new friends, help you learn more about the world, and give you amazing life experiences that will enrich your soul for years to come.

Start listing them out and counting them off as you go, making sure you've got them down. Just like my tweaking of *Ultraviolet*'s order of relationships, my categories are in this order for a reason, and I'll discuss that further on in the next few chapters as I give you tips and tricks to keep each finger's focus manageable.

Put all of these things together, and you'll not only organize your life quickly, but you'll feel better about how far you've already come.

Now, give yourself another high five—this chapter is complete!

QUICK SUMMARY:

- [ ] Your life is in your hands—literally.

- [ ] Five key areas to focus on for improvement are each represented by a finger:

  - **Thumb**: FAITH

  - **Pointer**: FAMILY & FRIENDS

  - **Middle**: FINANCES

  - **Ring**: FITNESS

  - **Pinky**: FUN

- [ ] Your identity touches all these areas of your life.

HIGH FIVES
ARE BETTER THAN
FACEPALMS

CHAPTER TWO
Thumbs Up

Life is Complicated

Life is complicated, and rightfully so—complicated things are harder to dismantle and discard.

But just because something is complicated, doesn't mean we can't break it down into simple parts.

And what better finger to start with than the thumb—the one that helps us break things apart?

Thumbs are unique in that they help us accomplish several functions.

Just like pandas have opposable thumbs to help them break up their bamboo, you have a thumb that can help you find the foundation of who you are.

That's why the first part of getting your life together is centered on the thumb of our hand model, which represents FAITH.

Why FAITH?

So many people do not understand what faith is.

Author, cultural commentator, and current atheist Richard Dawkins says, "Faith is the great cop-out, the great excuse to evade the need to think and evaluate evidence. Faith is the belief in spite of, even perhaps because of, the lack of evidence."

(Ironically, you need faith to believe he is right. This is a prime example of a self-defeating argument.)

On the other side, according to Hebrews 11:1, Biblical faith is, "the assurance of things hoped for, the conviction of things not seen," and further, it is a fruit of the Spirit (Galatians 5:22-23), and a gift from God (Ephesians 2:8-9).

And whether you believe in God or a higher power or not, here's the thing: No matter which definition you prefer, or which one you have for your own use, you have faith in *something*.

Everyone believes in something, even if it's nothing.

This is a universal idea behind character. Try writing a novel where the character's beliefs are wishy-washy, and you'll end up with a Gary Stu or Mary Sue before you finish the first chapter.

As a side note, one of the reasons I love the idea of God as the Grand Storyteller is because he knows how to write his characters.

There is a Japanese pop (J-pop) song I listened to back when I was a teenager called "White Destiny." It's from the *Prétear* anime series, and there's a line that's always stuck with me as an author:

> ***"Everything begins from the point of belief."***

As I started writing my stories, it struck me over and over again that the strongest parts of characters are their convictions—*good* characters, anyway.

And this speaks to us as people as much as it does for characters in a story.

Faith is the key to understanding our worldview; it tackles the "big questions" about life:

How did I get here?

What is your origin story?

Where does your life begin, and how does it intersect with others in your family, friends, and community?

How should I live?

What morals or rules will you live by that satisfy the demands you place on yourself—and do they apply to others, or only to yourself?

What kind of person do you want to be, and how do you want others to see you?

Where do I see meaning in my life?

What are the expectations you place on yourself regarding your choices and actions, and what is the complementary duty, sacrifice, work, or responsibility I must undertake to fulfill them?

What do you truly desire? What are some challenges you have already overcome?

What does success look like to you? What is the most important thing you want to accomplish in your life before you die?

What is my ultimate destiny?

How can I face death with dignity and see I have lived in a satisfactory manner?

All of these are questions that we ask ourselves, and all of the answers to these questions will eventually come out in the deeds that you do.

What you truly believe, others will see in what you do.

This means what you really believe—not just what you say you believe—will be clear from where you spend your time, how you prioritize your resources, and who you welcome into your circle of confidantes.

Back when I was a teacher, I often shared a quote—sometimes it is attributed to Lao Tzu, though it is also credited to Frank Outlaw—at the beginning of my classes:

"Watch your thoughts, they become words; watch your words, they become actions; watch your actions, they become habits; watch your habits, they become character; watch your character, for it becomes your destiny."

I always think of this when I think of how I want to live my life, and what kind of person I want to be, and what kind of person I am becoming.

FAITH in Action

What we believe about ourselves and our lives affects our actions, so when you count off on your thumb to help organize your life, you're checking to make sure that your actions match up with your beliefs.

For example, since I am a Christian, I believe in God, and I believe I need to prioritize prayer with God. So I will often ask myself, "Have I prayed today?"

And because I'm not always eager to be honest with myself, I'll usually follow that up with, "Did you really pay attention when you were praying?" The Lord knows I am easily distracted.

There are other things that are similar to this, like joining a prayer group, doing Bible studies, and journaling.

Many other faiths and religions have duties or suggested practices, and even secular humanistic science recommends meditation as a way to release stress.

Even broader beliefs can be transformed into meaningful actions.

If you believe you can make the world a better place, you can make it a weekly or daily practice to help someone out, give money to a cause you believe in, volunteer, give blood, do secret good deeds, or donate to a charity.

If you have been a victim of injustice, you can find a way to give justice or support to other people who have experienced similar atrocities.

If you know what it is like to be poor, hungry, lonely, or awkward, you can do your best to help someone who is struggling through those issues.

If you know how it feels to be overwhelmed by life and all its troubles, all at once, then you can write a book about how you survived it so others can find a lifeline in a time of turmoil—or you can just give them a copy of this book, of course.

Faith is a great way to offer yourself clarity about your life and its purpose; it gives meaning and beauty to the smallest actions you undertake, and it helps you not only push through hard times, but it adds to your joy when you face new challenges.

It is truly foundational to yourself and your life, and it helps you find others who share similar outlooks.

Faith is the key to making the world a better place—and that will make your life better, too.

What are you doing to show your faith today? This week? This month? Throughout your life?

Think it over, and then find actionable ways to show others what you believe. Choose at least one thing you believe—something deep and true—and take a small action this week to live it out.

And then give yourself a high five, because this chapter is over!

QUICK SUMMARY:

- [ ] Faith is foundational to your life, and it will affect everything else.

- [ ] Whether religious or not, everyone believes in something.

- [ ] Real belief shows up in your actions, not just your words.

- [ ] Big life questions (identity, purpose, and legacy) are rooted in what you believe.

- [ ] Reflect on what you truly believe—and how it guides your actions and shows others who you are on the inside.

HIGH FIVES
ARE BETTER THAN
FACEPALMS

CHAPTER THREE
Who's #1?

Life is Messy

Life is messy, and that's largely because it's full of messy people. You know this—you're one of them.

But just because something is messy, doesn't mean it can't be beautiful, and it doesn't have any meaning.

Much like fingers on a hand, people are both individuals and part of something greater.

We learn from each other, we need each other; and as much as you might hate people or hate the world, you need others in your life.

The nice thing about our messes is that they can often offer clues about how we can develop and nurture our relationships.

One of the first things I noticed as a teenager was that I was a lot better at solving other people's problems than my own; it was much easier to help other people get through their homework or clean their rooms than it was for me to take care of my own messes. This pattern has always repeated itself throughout my life.

One of the easiest ways to be happy is to make someone else happy, and one of the quickest ways to inspire yourself to get your life more organized is to help someone organize theirs.

Both religion and science have shown this relationship to be true.

In the Bible, The Golden Rule is to "treat others as you wish to be treated yourself," and to "Love your neighbor as yourself"—which means you must also love yourself as you would your neighbor.

Likewise, in his bestselling book, *Twelve Rules for Life*, Jordan B. Peterson explains how when we act as though we are responsible for ourselves like we were responsible for a pet or a friend, we have a better quality of life.

Some may ask, "How is helping someone else going to help me?" But helping others with their own messes and needs helps our own lives be more fulfilling.

This means that in life, to get more organized, you need to ask yourself, "Who is my #1?"

Family is the first foundation of our identity. Our parents give us our names, and names are the best way to describe the totality of who we are to others.

One of the best books on this idea of understanding the foundation of your life I've read is *Home Run: Learn God's Game Plan for Life and Leadership*, written by Kevin Myers and John C. Maxwell. The book goes through how we grow up and grow into ourselves.

Ideally, as we grow older, our family identity grows; we learn new skills, we try new things, and we experience life through our family's connections.

Once we're old enough and able enough to strike out independently, our friends further help us refine who we are. Friendships can form over similar interests, locations, values, and more, and just as it is important to know how to make friends, we also need to learn how to keep the good ones, and say goodbye to the bad ones.

Finally, as we grow, our community becomes the place where we give back and invest what we've been given.

This echoes the sentiment of Mother Theresa made during her Nobel Prize speech:

If you want to change the world, go home and love your family.

We change the world one person at a time, one moment at a time, and we're changed by the world throughout our time.

One of my other favorite quotes from Leo Tolstoy is, "Everyone thinks of changing the world, but no one thinks of changing himself."

In line with this, Gandhi is purported to have said, "Be the change you wish to see in the world."

We have tremendous power in choosing to take care of those we love, and letting them take care of us, too.

Loving on Your FAMILY & FRIENDS

Once you figure out who your #1 is, you count off your pointer finger and make sure you've made an effort (no matter how small or large) to take care of someone you love.

Much like our faith action, this can be something small.

You can give them a call, text them; send a gift. Even five minutes of your time is precious when it's a gift of love. You can cook dinner for them, plan vacations with them, or read a book together, play a game, or find a way to give them your time. I know more than one couple who share memes throughout their day. I have a friend who is homeschooling his sister so they can both spend more time with their grandfather. My own husband never hesitates to help fix things around my mom's house if she needs something done.

For my own personal habits for this, I usually try to check in with my family. This means calling them, texting them, or sometimes meeting them for lunch. If they're having a bad day, I listen, and sometimes I'll offer to help if I can.

There are other ways to help, too. You can help someone physically (Does your neighbor need her lawn mowed?), mentally (Can you listen to a friend talk about a problem over coffee?), financially (Can you buy that homeless person some socks and some oranges?), and relationally (Can you thank a friend for your friendship in the past, or maybe plan a reunion in the future?).

It doesn't have to be big—although it can be. It just has to be genuine and as consistent as you can make it.

We live in a world that's largely pragmatic with everything and more, but you shouldn't be pragmatic with people. They aren't problems to solve or investments to manage. They're gifts you ought to take care of.

When my kids visit our relatives, I've trained them not to get hooked on the screens that might herald them; I've told them more than once, and loud enough my mother-in-law can hear me that "These are the people that if you die, God forbid, they're going to show up to your funeral. You don't want them to only remember how you'd visit them for their video games or cable TV. We're here to visit *people*, not their stuff."

My kids just kind of roll their eyes, and I usually get some odd looks if the relatives in question haven't heard me say it before.

But it's the truth.

If you love someone, you'll do your best to take care of them.

Think about who your heart points to when you think of someone you love.

Write down a daily or weekly goal, or even just one big goal you'd like to do for them. If you're having trouble thinking of something, consider checking over the Maslow's Hierarchy of Needs pyramid; this walks you through the things people need to survive (such as food, clothes, being able to poo), all the ways up to the things that help people thrive, like trustworthy relationships, health, confidence, accountability, and the chance to feel as though they've become the people they were meant to be.

Remembering your family and friends (your found family, if you will) also shows you are reliable—and even if your own life is still messy, you have people cheering you on, and you'll be able to do the same for them. When we have family, we have a place where we can truly grow and take on our goals, knowing people we love and trust are there for us when we need encouragement.

So, now then, answer this question: Who's your #1 today—and how will you show them they matter?

Once you've done that, give yourself another high five—that's all for this chapter!

QUICK SUMMARY:

- [ ] Life is messy because people are messy—but that's not a bad thing.

- [ ] Our relationships shape us: Family gives us roots, while friends give us refinement, and community gives us purpose.

- [ ] Loving others is one of the best ways to improve your own life.

- [ ] Even smaller acts that show how we care for others (calls, texts, quality time) matter.

- [ ] Treat people as gifts, not obligations or distractions.

- [ ] Reflect on who are the people most important to you, and how are you showing them they matter? What is something you can do to show you're taking care of them?

HIGH FIVES
ARE BETTER THAN
FACEPALMS

CHAPTER FOUR

Give Your Finances the Bird

Life is Rewarding

Life is rewarding, but if you want to see the financial benefits of it, you're going to have to pay close attention. This is where a lot of training comes in, requiring you to put in the work and make sacrifices.

Many people—perhaps too many—use money as a measurement for success. Others use it as their lives' primary goal and pursuit.

But money is more like the superhero serum for Captain America: It's not inherently good or evil in its own right. It simply makes you more of what you are already.

It's a tool that we use, for good or ill, and whether we have a good grasp of how to handle it or not, it will affect our lives in some manner.

With this in mind, you need to organize your money if you're going to organize your life, and that means you're going to have to control your money.

America's leading financial expert, Dave Ramsey, says, "You have to control your money, or your money will control you."

Like before, when you did a mental inventory of your beliefs and your family and friends, you'll need to know where your money is, how much you have, and what you may owe to others. You should also know about how much you spend to stay alive and/or comfortable.

You should have an idea of what you'd like to do with money. Once you decide on what you'd like to do with your money, it's easier to start organizing it.

Some people need to get out of debt, for example. Others want to invest. More want to save up to start their own business, or they want to go to college.

There are so many books and other resources on money, it's like walking into a minefield. There are books, courses, videos, and influencers who all peddle their financial philosophies.

In his bestselling book, *I Will Teach You to Be Rich,* Ramit Sethi makes the comparison of dealing with finances to being healthy. Most people need to make more money than they spend, just like people need to make sure they're burning more calories than they eat.

For this chapter, I recommend figuring out what you want out of life that you'll need money to get—those new tech gadgets, new car, and summer vacation aren't going to pay for itself, and neither is that Ferrari or goat farm—and then working on saving more than you spend.

You can do more things with money that require CPA knowledge and Financial Planner insight if you actually have more money.

Personally, when I first jumped on my own High Fives are better than Facepalms journey here, I was more concerned with getting out of debt than anything else.

When I was younger, my parents told me that I would "never be without debt," and I think my teenage mind set out to prove them wrong. Maybe they did it on purpose, to help me move away from my unhealthy spending habits.

I'm old enough now, and wise enough, to know you can absolutely live without debt, and it's a goal worth striving for, even if it's hard.

While I still have to cut down my mortgage, I will say checking off my to-do list with my middle finger as I put money down on my debt makes me feel like Batman locking up the Joker each week: My mental foe is subdued, even if he is still laughing at me; but I can breathe a little better knowing he is out of the way for a while.

I feel every syllable of pain when Dave Ramsey says, "The Bible says 'the borrower is slave to the lender.'"

That's why out of all my recommendations, I would suggest checking out Dave Ramsey's *Financial Peace University* the most. This is the most comprehensive, user-friendly for getting out of debt, getting financially secure, and planning for retirement. I like the system because it has a lot of help for different problems and steps to help beginners as well as savvy seasoned financial planners.

FINANCIAL Rewards

One of the nicest things about money is that you can physically see it as you collect it—or you can see your debt go down as you pay it off.

If you do anything extra-special with your money, such as working on tithing regularly, investing in a friend's dream, or donating to a charity you believe in, you can also easily keep track of this.

The best thing for this chapter is to think of what you need to do with your finances—save, give, or pay off debt—and develop a goal for yourself.

The hardest part about money is that we usually have more than one thing going on at one time; it's good to budget and save, it's good to pay down debt, and it's good to put your money where your beliefs are.

Right now, what's one thing you can do this week to move closer to your financial goals—save, give, or pay off?

Once you figure out what you have, and what you need to do, write down some specific goals you have for your money, and then, as you go throughout your days and weeks, check in with your middle finger to make sure you're doing a flipping good job on managing your finances.

Now, treat yourself to another high five—that's the end of this chapter!

QUICK SUMMARY:

- [ ] Money isn't the goal—it's a tool that magnifies who you already are.

- [ ] Organizing your money helps you organize your life.

- [ ] Know where your money is, what you owe, and what you want your money to do for you.

- [ ] Getting out of debt is one of the fastest ways to gain financial peace and control. What's one goal you have for your money that you can do? Write it down where you'll see it every week, and make sure you're checking in periodically.

HIGH FIVES
ARE BETTER THAN
FACEPALMS

C. S. JOHNSON

CHAPTER FIVE
Put a Ring on Your Fitness Routine

Life is Beautiful

Life is beautiful, even when you don't feel particularly beautiful.

Imagine everything that went into making the current moment of your life—all the moments, the seconds, all the people and their choices, all the strange events, all the different twists and turns of time and space; all of the struggles and the second chances and the sudden changes; all the sacrifice and wishing and dreaming and hoping—all of it. There are infinite numbers of decisions and words and thoughts and people that have led you to this current moment in time.

Einstein is thought to have made the comment, "There are only two ways to live your life. One is as though nothing is a miracle. The other is as though everything is a miracle."

In the graphic comic series, *Watchmen*, Dr. Manhattan makes a similar observation when he and Laurie, Silk Specter's daughter, are talking on Mars. There, Dr. Manhattan is struggling to find empathy for humanity, after decades of detachment and "otherness" from humanity, caused by the lab explosion he experienced. As Laurie realizes her father is The Comedian, a man who had assaulted and her mother initially despised, Dr. Manhattan, recognizing the overwhelming unlikeliness of her existence. He says, "The existence of life is a highly overrated phenomenon ... But your life, the complexity of it ... the sheer improbability ... is a miracle."

And Laurie is not the only one like that. I am a miracle, and you are, too.

Because of this, life is beautiful, even if it's messy and uncertain at times.

My kids are getting older, and as we're getting closer to the puberty years, I tell them—especially my daughter—that puberty years are like the "cocoon" years. We've raised butterflies a few times, so there are a lot of ugly caterpillars on the ground now, and when I see them, even though they're ugly now, they'll be in their cocoons soon, and then, after that, they'll be beautiful butterflies.

I like this metaphor; butterflies spend over half their lives ugly first, though, and they only get their wings as large as they do by struggling to get free of their cocoon, something they'd built to protect themselves while they change.

Of course, there are some things that likely won't change.

When I was younger, I was made fun of for any number of things—we're very rarely as smart, funny, pretty, thin, or ambitious as others want us to be when we're young—but I remember a lot of teasing about my nose. It's a very clearly Eastern European nose, from my father's side of the family, and it's at odds with my Western European heritage from my mom's side of the family.

Now, as a mother, I have my kids, and even with a subscription to a Plastic Surgery+ app (trademark pending, no doubt, ha!), no amount of nose jobs is going to change my genes. At that point, it became my responsibility to get over my insecurities, so I will then be able to teach my kids to do the same if it happens.

I say this because much about getting healthy and becoming beautiful is the same, but here, when I say "beautiful," I mean healthy, confident in your value, and understanding you have been given responsibility for yourself, and you're working on being the best you that you can be.

Some of that is cheesy-sounding, but who wouldn't say no to a little extra cheese on their pizza? And even if you would, Garfield the cat wouldn't, and not the Teenage Mutant Ninja Turtles. And neither would a lot of the people I know, and likely not a lot of the people you know, too.

So there are plenty of people who will love you and people you will love who will see the cheese in those statements and love you all the more for them.

On a more serious note, people can *be* healthy and *feel* beautiful at the same time. It is the ideal. No one would choose just one of those things when they can have both.

Finding FITNESS Goals for You

Much like your finances, you'll need to start thinking about what you want out of your fitness goals, and then break them down into small, manageable, tangible, realistic, and fun. It's much easier to make it a type of game, or find a good fitness program that you can do with friends or a group, if you think that will be more fun.

'Fitness' is a broad topic, so be sure to break it down as needed. More specific goals about your nutrition, fitness, stress management, cleanliness, and life-balance are key. Your body is designed a certain way, and you need to be able to work with it to optimize your life.

One of my daily goals every day is to take my vitamins. I didn't like this as a kid, but now that I'm older, I especially like taking my supplements since I know I don't eat enough of the right foods to get all the ones I need.

And yes, I still don't really like doing this every day. It's definitely not "fun," but it's better than the not-fun of facing the inevitable consequences of joint pain, digestion issues, or malnutrition.

Another fitness goal I have is to walk more. Walking is just a great way overall to relieve my stress, so it's helpful on both physical and mental levels.

One of the big ones I've started doing since my mid-thirties is to get enough sleep. Sadly, I'm definitely not young enough not to feel sleep deprived if I get less than eight hours anymore.

Since you're able to tailor your approach to overall health and wellness, write down a few goals you have. Maybe it's to lose weight or gain muscle, increase your strength or flexibility or your stamina; maybe it's to eat better, learn to cook healthier food, stay away from too many sweets, take your vitamins; maybe it's to work up to running a marathon, or getting involved with a local sports league, or taking up karate or Pilates or weight-lifting. The key to success here is just trying, and committing to keep trying.

Get your list ready: Think of things you'll do this week to strengthen your health—physically, mentally, or emotionally—and then write them down and keep yourself accountable.

Your body, just like your hand and your name, is a representation of your whole self. How you look is only part of that, and if you want to feel better and look better, finding a good fitness routine is a great place to start!

And give yourself a small workout now by giving yourself a high five—this chapter's over!

QUICK SUMMARY:

- [ ] Your life is full of meaning and beauty—even when you don't feel like it does.

- [ ] Transformation takes time. Like a butterfly in a cocoon, becoming your healthiest self involves struggle, growth, and patience.

- [ ] Self-esteem is not the same thing as confidence; you can lie to yourself, but you can't hide what others see. Being confident means being able to list times when others saw you stick with your commitments, even when it was hard.

- [ ] Small, realistic goals make a big difference. From walking daily to taking your vitamins or getting more sleep, success comes from consistent, manageable actions. And don't be afraid to update or change a goal that's not working for you—not to be confused with you not working for it, of course!

- [ ] Your body reflects the care you put into your life. It's not just about how you look—it's how you feel, how you function, and how you honor the gift of being alive.

CHAPTER SIX
Pinkie Promise

Life is FUN

Life is *fun*.

Really.

Think about it—you don't see any dead people riding on roller coasters, sunbathing at the beach, climbing a mountain, watching a favorite movie, reading great books, playing with their pets, winning awards, designing new buildings, drawing up new blueprints, eating tasty food, or throwing parties.

At least as long as you're not pulling a *Weekend at Bernie's* kind of prank.

Speaking of which, when I say "fun," I mean good, wholesome fun. I'm not talking about an addiction or abuse that's been marketed as "fun."

Real fun empowers you to feel virtuous joy—a sense of contentment and completion that resonates down in your soul.

One of the reasons I think the devil goes after fun is that too much of it will consume you inside and out, and too little of it will drain you into soulful starvation.

So many of our virtues and vices have to be balanced out. Too little, and we suffer, and often take others down with us; yet, too much, and we suffer, and we often take others up and over the moon, only to crash out with us, too.

In this fallen world, there will always be trouble—but there will always be chances to turn those troubles into opportunities to learn new things; they can be new things about yourself, and new adventures you'd like to have.

Even when you're stressed out, sometimes taking a little break for some fun can really make a difference in your life, and even a little fun—speaking of your littlest finger here for good reason—is good for you to prioritize.

There's a reason stressed-out people die earlier on average.

Pinky Promise Yourself FUN

Yes, pinky promise yourself that you will find something fun you love, and chase after it as you seek to organize the rest of your life.

Think of something this week that you find fun, and figure out a goal for it. For example, I like to write (if you didn't notice yet), so I try to write something every day. I also like to travel, so I like to plan out vacations with my family. Husband enjoys this, too, since it's a nice break from work stress for him, and it's a great way for us to spend time together as a family. Even just planning it gives us something to talk about with our kids and each other.

The first big caveat with the fun in your life is just to make sure you don't compromise on your other goals (too much) to get it. If you're stuck in debt, buying a new car for "fun" isn't wise. If you're trying to lose weight, taste-testing all the ice cream pints at your local ice cream shop isn't a good idea.

And then the second caveat with fun is that you shouldn't worry about what other people think of you for it. These should be fun things that you do, even if no one else understands why you want to do them.

You don't have to monetize it.

You don't have to share it.

You don't have to justify it to yourself.

You're already working hard to make your life better. More challenges will come in the future. So for now, don't let all the bad things in your life make you forget about all the good—that just ensures that the bad things in the world will win against you.

Life is hard. Life is complicated. Life is rewarding. Life is beautiful.

And yes, life is fun!

High fives all around!

QUICK SUMMARY:

- [ ] It's more than okay to focus on your hobbies, and learning how to embrace healthy fun is essential for your overall well-being.

- [ ] Fun helps you recharge and reconnects you to both others and yourself.

- [ ] Don't forget to factor your fun in with the other goals you have so it doesn't overshadow your other priorities or get buried in a to-do list that makes you burnout.

CONCLUSION
One Last High Five!

Life is What You Make of It

Life is crazy, but you don't have to be—and more importantly, you *shouldn't* want to be crazy.

Life is what you make of it—so make it count. You don't have to be perfect, just persistent and present. Keep pursuing a more intentional, joy-filled life.

Throughout this short book, I've given real-life examples from my own life, as well as some from others. I also recommend all the books I've talked about or mentioned (to adults; some parents may want to hold off on some of them, at their discretion), and I'd like to insist here that audiobooks still count, too, but get the physical media if you enjoy it.

One thing last thing I'd like to recommend before you go is Habitica.

We live in a game-saturated world, and "gamification" can really help your progress. I've used Habitica for several years to help keep me on target for my to-do list. I don't use the social media or messaging features for it outside my family, and I'm not an affiliate, but even if I'm not paid for it, so far I love their app and recommend it.

https://habitica.com/

And with that said …

That's all folks!

Give yourself one last high five—because you've come to the end of this book!

HIGH FIVES
ARE BETTER THAN
FACEPALMS

C. S. JOHNSON

REFERENCES

Berg, E. (2021, May 22). *How to turn your stress to zero* [Video]. YouTube. https://www.youtube.com/watch?v=U5odrIsm-60

Einstein, A. (attributed). (2024). *Everything is a miracle* [Quote]. Quote Investigator. https://quoteinvestigator.com/2024/05/04/everything-miracle/

Habitica. (n.d.). *Habitica: Gamify your life.* https://habitica.com/

Lewis, C. S. (2001). *Mere Christianity.* HarperOne. (Original work published 1952)

Lucado, M. (2005). *Cure for the common life: Living in your sweet spot.* Thomas Nelson.

McLeod, S. (2023). *Maslow's hierarchy of needs.* Simply Psychology. https://www.simplypsychology.org/maslow.html

Meyers, K., & Maxwell, J. C. (2014). *Home run: Learn God's game plan for life and leadership.* Thomas Nelson.

Mother Teresa. (1979). *If you want to change the world, go home and love your family* [Quote]. See also: Wake Up Call. (2016, May 17). *Advice from Mother Teresa on making your world a better place.* Patheos. https://www.patheos.com/blogs/wakeup call/2016/05/advice-from-mother-teresa-on-making-your-world-a-better-place/

Outlaw, F. (n.d.). *Watch your thoughts, they become words...* [Quote]. Goodreads. https://www.goodreads.com/quotes/650 7450-watch-your-thoughts-they-become-w ords-watch-your-words-they

Peterson, J. B. (2018). *12 rules for life: An antidote to chaos.* Random House Canada.

Tan, A. (2001). *The bonesetter's daughter.* Putnam.

The Holy Bible, English Standard Version. (2001). Crossway Bibles. (Original work published ca. 1000 B.C.–100 A.D.)

The Myers & Briggs Foundation. (n.d.). *The Myers-Briggs type indicator.* https://www.myersbriggs.org

Truity. (n.d.). *The big five personality test.* https://www.truity.com/test/big-five-personality-test

Ultraviolet. Wimmer, K. (Director). (2006). *Ultraviolet* [Film]. Screen Gems.

Watchmen. Moore, A., & Gibbons, D. (1986–1987). *Watchmen.* DC Comics.

White Destiny. (2001). *Opening theme of Prétear* [Song]. Performed by Yoko Ishida. King Records.

123test. (n.d.). *The DISC personality test.* https://www.123test.com/disc-personality-test/

C. S. JOHNSON

AUTHOR'S NOTE

Dear Reader,

First of all, I wanted to thank you for reaching this far into the book. I realize in a world of constant, endless advertisements and perpetual demands on your time, it's easy and perhaps even preferable for you to overlook this small book of mine.

Second of all, because this is my book, and I'm my own publisher, I wanted to take this chance to say that while you're here to organize your life, you ought to be a Christian.

While I worked through the many questions you have to ask yourself to organize your life, the biggest one we all actually face is the question of "What will you do with God?"

In the course of my own life, I have walked with God long enough to know my own soul's pitfalls, but also the salvation in His Grace. I've been fortunate to have had great mentors, fabulous examples, and solid, Bible-believing churches that have nurtured me and helped me grow in Christ. I've also met many people who have had the opposite of that.

You may have met Christians before that have failed you, hurt you, abused you;

Christians that left you bitter, left you disappointed and depressed, left you angry, or maybe just plain left you.

I can't apologize for that—not in a way that's meaningful to you, anyway. But I would like to gently point out that Christians are still fallen humans, and the Bible tells us that there will be some who say they are believers, but they are lying, or they are fooling themselves, or it's possible they're newer Christians, who haven't been with the church long enough to teach others effectively about the faith.

Please do not let these people who have decimated your soul damage you even more by letting their picture be the one you see in your mind when you think of all Christians.

I would encourage you instead to think of Jesus. He, too, was hurt, disappointed, left alone, lied to, betrayed, and abused. He was perfect, sinless, but he was still sent to die. He is the ultimate embodiment, literally, of God and the perfect model for our lives.

Starting with Jesus is great for finding information, too. Some people, while not traumatized away from Christ, just don't feel they have enough information on it to make a decision to commit their lives to him. The best place for you to begin here that I would recommend is *Mere Christianity*, which was written in the 1940s by C. S. Lewis, and broadcast over the radio waves during WWII's London bombings. In the book, Lewis goes through the reasons he, as a former atheist, hated God, and also why Christianity was not as unreasonable as he'd first believed, and a lot of the basics of Christian teaching and Christian thought. He has a lot to say about the Moral Law and why the Christian virtues are indeed virtuous.

There are many other things to say—the cosmological argument for God, which states everything that has a beginning has a cause, which makes it begin to exist; the teleological argument, which says that because the universe exhibits order, purpose, and complexity, it suggests it was designed, and by an intelligent designer; there's the ontological stance, where because God is idealized as the greatest good that could ever be conceived—but science came out of Christians believing in a God capable of rational thought, and that his universe would reflect that, and now it is sustained by that paradigm, even if many do not see him directly in their studies. There is also the matter of the reliability of the Bible—a 99.5% historicity rate, where no major doctrines of Christianity are in dispute—and the unreliability of comparable texts, aside from the Hebrew's Old Testament.

Yes, there are many other things to say.

But at the end of all things, the same question remains:

"What will you do with God?"

I hope, like the other questions I've asked in this book, you will carefully consider your answer, and seek it out, even if it's uncomfortable. If you'd like to pray, all it starts with is, "Dear God," and you get to fill in the rest. I believe in the Bible and in Jesus, and I know he's already died for you. I have full faith he's winning to do what it takes to meet you where you're at. All you need to do is give him that opportunity and embrace it.

I tell my kids that I hope they get the best of me. My son has my heart, his daddy's hands, and a mind of his own. My daughter is my shadow and my light; one day, I will burn out, and she will shine with both our fire. But even after all this, I want them to have my faith. I know that my faith in Jesus is the only reason I'm alive today, and he's the only reason I have all the blessings and miracles in my life that I do. How could I not love someone who loves me so pervasively and profusely, even after all the trouble I've caused?

And that's why I'd like you to find him, too. That's really all I had to say about it here.

If you are still reading this, I am praying for you to find him today, and I wish you all the best.

These things I pray in Jesus' name, amen.

Until We Meet Again,

C. S. Johnson

C. S. Johnson is the award-winning, genre-hopping author of several novels, including young adult sci-fi and fantasy adventures such as the Starlight Chronicles series, the Once Upon a Princess saga, and the Divine Space Pirates trilogy. She has also contributed articles around the internet at StudioJakeMedia, HollywoodinToto, The Rebelution, and MTL Magazine. With a gift for sarcasm and an apologetic heart, she currently lives in Atlanta with her family. Visit www.csjohnson.me for more.

Since I also write fiction, please read on ahead for a sample chapter of my other work!

C. S. JOHNSON

AUTHOR ACKNOWLEDGEMENTS

This book, as with all my work, is dedicated to my supporters. In the last decade-plus of my publishing career, I have known some truly fabulous people, and they have been kind and generous enough to support me in various ways, even when I wasn't sure of where I was going or how I was figuring things out.

I am sincerely thankful for all my Ko-Fi supporters, my Substack readers, and my (Almost) Famous Readers. Each person I have been able to help, inspire, or assist in some way through my work is because of those who have supported me. God bless you all, and may you have all the best.

Until We Meet Again,

C. S. Johnson

CSJohnson x

C. S. JOHNSON

C. S. JOHNSON

SAMPLE READING

Chapter 1 *from*

KITSUNEKO

A COMPANION NOVELLA TO

THE REALMS BEYOND THE RAINBOW

※   ※   ※   ※

C. S. Johnson

C. S. JOHNSON

CHAPTER ONE

※　　※　　※　　※

I look in the mirror carefully, scrutinizing the smallest details of the face before me. It is the face of a beautiful young woman, serene and striking all at once. I study the rosy cheeks, still youthfully plump while they start to hint at adulthood, while golden hair falls to either side, sweeping long past the pointed chin. My focus fastens onto the nose in wonderment, mesmerized by the size of the little bump that turns up at its end. I press down on it with my finger, and it shrinks, ever so slightly, in size.

Finally, my gaze travels to see the two large, slanted eyes staring back at me; the misty green twinkles, simultaneously bewildered and cautious.

The eyes are mine, even if the rest of the face is not.

Of all the different kinds of changelings, the kitsunefolk are the only ones whose eyes refuse to change. I doubt this is anything but by design; my kinfolk are known for their inner stubbornness as much as they are known for their outward flexibility. Add in the catblood, and that's me.

I am a changeling from the Honeyspice Lands, a kitsune-neko, and that's all. That is my only role to play in the grand kingdom of Toulacoeur, and so much so, that's what they named me.

I am Kitsuneko, slave of King Dario and his wife, Queen Arianna, their full-time substitute for their daughter, Princess Cari.

I smile into the mirror, and the face of Princess Cari smiles back at me.

"Perfect," I whisper. "You look just like her."

Or at least, I look like what most people think Princess Cari would look like, if she hadn't been kidnapped seventeen years ago.

"Well, where is she? Isn't she ready yet?"

The anxious voice of the queen cuts through my concentration; my pointed, black-tipped ears, the ears of a fox-cat changeling, suddenly shoot out of either side of my head, instinctively twitching and shuddering. I watch with remorse, and only a little bit of prideful cheer, as the blonde hair of the princess changes to my usual shade of reddish brown.

I touch the ears and rub them, praying to the god of Toulacoeur for comfort. I don't know if he hears me, but there is an unspeakable sense of peace that settles around me. Calm once more, my ears slip back into my head, and I am able to hold my transformation.

A small sigh escapes me. I've always been a good changeling—my very life and its quality depends on it, after all—but no matter my level of skill or the amount of time I practice, there are always some moments I can't control it, especially when I am alone.

Perhaps after all the time I have spent covering up, I owe it to myself to figure out just who it is I am erasing.

Back in the mirror, the princess's shapely lips curve into a dark, wry smile as my ears begin to slip back into Cari's crown of golden locks. *Or perhaps it is good that the king and queen don't allow me to be alone very often then, hmm?*

It's not as if I am the only changeling in the world able to mimic Princess Cari's likeness; I was just the most convenient one around when they conscripted me into service, and I will be quickly disposed of if I become inconvenient.

Almost as if they can hear my thoughts, the door swings open. I suck in my breath and squeeze my eyes shut, allowing myself one last second to myself, before facing the inevitable.

"Kitty?"

My breath leaves me in one long exhale, and I almost giggle at my happy turn of fate. "Lights above, Kiro, I thought you were your mother."

"You mean 'our mother,' don't you?" My pretend brother's teasing tone is light, but I know just from looking at him that despite his smile, he is struggling just as much as I am.

His eyes narrow he looks around my room.

"No one else is here," I tell him, and I can see this is what he wants to hear. His shoulders relax, if only momentarily.

We are children of the king and queen, and our privacy is as rare to us as gold to the poorest of the poor.

"I guess there are no festivities today, other than dancing and eating? I can't imagine you'd be allowed to wear that otherwise," I say, pointing to his spiderfly silk shirt and the rich brocade of his vest as I try lightening his mood a little more.

"Of course not. The king and queen never bother themselves with what I want, not even at my birthday ball."

I reach over and pull him into what is supposed to be a quick hug. "It'll be fine in the end. It's only for one night, after all. We can go on one of our secret adventures tomorrow, if that will make you feel better."

For the past several years, Kiro and I have indulged ourselves in different outings, from exploring the hidden rooms of the palace, to secret picnics—even sneaking into the city in disguise. We aren't able to do them very often, not without risking anger from the king and queen or discovery by the guards or the citizens. But I feel it is worth the hazard, if it will only make Kiro happy.

Kiro says nothing as he continues to embrace me.

My breath catches in my throat. It doesn't matter how many times he's held me before, I am always surprised at Kiro's gentleness. With his broad shoulders and narrow hips, Kiro is a perfect mirror to the king and his legacy as a legendary warrior. He is much taller than me, even with the illusion of Cari's height. His hair is the color of warm moonlight, while his blue eyes, bright with intelligence and laughter, gaze past the barriers of our world.

While I have learned beside him or followed behind him nearly all my life, Kiro has always been my best friend and only confidante. I know him better than I even know myself. He is not the only one who knows I am not really his sister, but he is the only one who never held it against me. Every kindness he has ever shown me, I have harbored in my memory, using that collection as a bulwark to keep back the sad weariness of his mother's depression or his father's oppressive neglect.

I wonder at how well I fit in his arms, even if it is no wonder to me that I am in love with him.

At that thought, I pull back from him, more than a little reluctantly. He is still nervous, and I suppose I can't blame him.

Tonight is the night of his twentieth birthday ball. Kiro is now of age to inherit the kingdom, should the king abdicate, or if something else should happen. He is the future, and the future is secure; everyone in the kingdom is excited for him.

Everyone, of course, except me.

But just as I pretend to be his older sister, I put on a false smile and pretend to be happy for him tonight.

I owe him too much to want to tell him the truth.

"Mother wants to know if you're ready for tonight, if you haven't already heard," Kiro says. This time, his voice is more restrained, and I know it's time to concern ourselves with our duties.

He has always been a good son, and I have always done my best to fulfill my duty, too.

"Of course," I agreed, switching my voice to mimic the queen's accent and standing up straighter. "I was just finishing up. You know, making sure everything's in the right place."

"Unless my sister ever returns to Toulacoeur, we'll never know what's supposed to be the right place." He scoffs. "I like you better when it's *really* you, Kitty."

My heart both leaps and falls at his moment of honesty, and I swallow hard, knowing it will be even more difficult for me to make it through the night.

"I could look like you, if you think that would be better," I say, already reworking my face to look like his. It takes me only a few seconds to transform my face perfectly into his, other than the eyes, and when I scowl at him in play, he finally laughs.

"Cari's face is better suited to your dress than mine," Kiro says. "Remind me to never make you mad."

"Yes, somehow I don't think the king's guards would let you forget it if they saw you in this," I agree. The gown the queen had sent up earlier was very beautiful; it was a fine, silvery gray, like a raincloud about to burst. The long sleeves and square neckline, together with the high waist, made me feel taller as much as it made me look older. I tugged at the long skirt, showing off its fullness. I let my face resume its impression of Cari as I playfully twirl around. "Still, it's very lovely. I think it's a good sign that the silk trade agreements are still going strong among the realms, right?"

When I look up, I see Kiro is staring intently at me, in such a way that stops my heart as much as it makes it beat faster.

Before I can say anything—before I can breathe properly again—he frowns and nods. "You'll pass for Cari, as usual."

"No need to say it so sullenly," I say. "I like to think my talent has improved over the years."

"It needed to, with all your growth spurts." Kiro slips around me, grabbing my hand and leading me into another spin. "You're not sporting a tail this time, are you?"

"No." I grab at the back of the gown they'd sent me, the smoothness of its finery easily making my hands slip around my backside. There is no tail, fortunately, and I hate how relieved I feel. I whirl around so Kiro can't see, but as I turn, in that second, I catch his gaze lingering on my body, and I blush. The heat on my cheeks burns even more as Kiro clears his throat.

"Well, that's good," he says. "I remember when that happened at your last birthday, the queen spent a good two weeks in her bed while the king just raged whenever someone mentioned your 'foolish prank.'"

I don't say anything. I do not want to remind him of the days following that episode. After the king had chastised me, threatening me with whippings and even imprisonment, I'd been scared to leave my room. Two days had passed as I starved, before Kiro had shown up at my door with an armful of pilfered treats from the kitchen.

The kingdom is in a tenuous enough position. Rumors of Cari's kidnapping have never fully disappeared; I know there is speculation among the population that I am an imposter, a child the king and queen adopted to take Cari's place.

It isn't the truth, but it is too close for comfort.

I had been too young to remember everything myself, only that the princess's disappearance was upsetting and dangerous; of course, at the time, I'd only just arrived at the palace myself. I'd been a gift for the king and queen from an ambassador from the Honeyspice Lands, one who claimed he'd found me as a stowaway in one of his spice warehouses. I was three years old at the time, and my changeling abilities were just starting to allow me to look fully human.

Even all these years later, things are still bad enough, with the queen's health failing drastically, and the other realms starting to doubt the unity Toulacoeur's legacy offered. Kiro's birthday today was a mark in securing the kingdom's rule, even if the question of its protection remained uncertain.

"Well, let's go and get this over with." Kiro puts his hand on my arm. The strength I feel in him is thoughtfully restrained, and I lean into his softness. We stand there together, and it is only when I notice that he hasn't moved that I tug on his sleeve.

"Your mother—*our* mother—is waiting," I say.

He still doesn't move, and then he looks at me again. His blue eyes are mesmerizing; a second later, all the work I'd put into looking like Princess Cari is undone. My auburn hair overtakes the golden locks, the white lines that outline my eyes strike out like silver, and my pointed ears slip out once more. My cheeks are full of fire as I realize what's happened, and I try to pull back, embarrassed.

"No. Kitty, wait." Kiro doesn't let me move. The way he speaks my name is a symphony, his voice full of a richness and beauty that instantly captivates me, and I am lost as I stare back at him.

He brushes a strand of my hair away from my eyes. "I know it's the wrong time to tell you this … but … I … "

He steps closer and begins to lean toward me, bringing his mouth closer to mine. I feel the tremor of the earth inside of me as I realize he is going to kiss me, and there is nothing in me, not even my sense of duty, that will move to stop him.

I want him to kiss me, too.

My eyes close as my heart thunders between my ears, and I taste his breath as it mingles with mine.

Our lips are just about to touch as the hardened voice of Queen Arianna screeches between us.

"Kitsuneko, by all that is bright, where *are* you? The procession is leaving the castle!"

My eyes shoot open, and my trembling body jerks back out of Kiro's reach. The queen's anger is a weapon, a sword that remains sharp by its rare use more than its refining. Her voice summons back my common sense, reminding me more forcefully than ever I am only alive at her good will.

The absolutely last thing she would want is to find out I am in love with Kiro. That would be too inconvenient, not just for her, but for everyone else in the kingdom.

"I'm coming," I holler back, still blushing furiously but desperate to correct my outward features.

Kiro is surprised as much as I am, but thanks to his years training in the king's guard, he is able to hide it better. If I did not know him so well, I would have missed the nervous, angry way he ran his hand through his hair.

The door opens, and one of the queen's handmaidens, Juni, comes in. She really should be called a "hand-matron," considering her old age. In many ways, she is like the queen's mother, having been her nursemaid and later her first official handmaiden.

But despite her closeness to the queen, I like Juni. She is the one who calls me "Honeyspice," and just like Kiro calling me "Kitty," I feel a special bond with her because of it. She serves as a mother-figure to me, especially when the queen is too distraught to even look my way. Juni has watched over me and Kiro when, in our younger days, we would run through the palace gardens or go riding throughout Toulacoeur's capital, Auralis. Even then, I knew her softness as much as her sternness, and I was comforted that there was never one without an inkling of the other.

"Oh, Honeyspice," she coos, easily pushing past Kiro as she begins to paw at my gown. "You need to get moving. My Ari's fretting."

I nod frantically. "I was—"

"Just getting me to make sure she was all set," Kiro interrupts. "I'll go and tell Mother she doesn't need to worry so."

"Bangs, please," Juni orders me, parting my now-golden hair off to the side. I shorten the front to please her before she turns to give Kiro a skeptical smile. "I've been telling her that for years, Highness, and there's no point in pretending it helps. She's looking for a white unicorn to come riding over the horizon, and she won't be satisfied until she sees him again."

"True enough," Kiro agrees. He turns to me, his eyes still blazing with intensity. "We'll finish our conversation later."

I say nothing, only nodding and giving him an awkward half-smile as he leaves my room. My tongue is too thick and my pride is too scared to say anything else.

Juni distracts me at once, tugging on the train of my dress and checking the fit of my bodice.

"You need to be an inch taller," she says. "Cari is twenty-two now. She's past full-grown, I would imagine."

There's a sadness in her voice that carries over into my own heart. Princess Cari has grown up, assuming she survived, without her mother or her father and without her brother. There was no way to know what kind of life she'd lived since she'd been lost.

I am grateful I am at least able to have Kiro, though I wonder, as I think of how sure I'd been that he wanted to kiss me, how much longer my time with him will be.

Kiro and I will never be able to be together. He is a prince, and I am a slave.

"One last thing, and you'll be ready," Juni says. "Ari told me to make sure you wear Kleon's tiara."

"The Unicorn tiara?"

Juni nods firmly, trying to reassure my uncertainty. "Yes, Honeyspice," she says softly. "Tonight's an important night."

"I know." I swallow hard and try to look happy as Juni goes over to my jewelry cabinets and pulls out a chatelaine of keys. "Kiro's birthday is always fun for the kingdom to celebrate. I am sure now that he is old enough to take the throne, the people will be extra enthusiastic."

"That's not all we'll be celebrating tonight." Juni turns the key and unlocks the drawer, pulling out the Unicorn tiara.

I've only worn it once before, on Cari's twentieth birthday celebration two years before. It is the crown of the Unicorn's Keeper, a duty which has been passed down from daughter to daughter since the Seven Realms of the Rainbow was united by the first king, eleven generations before. He was the one who conquered all the realms with the blessing of Kleon the Unicorn, and from that point on, the seven realms have been at peace.

I gulp as Juni places the tiara on my head. I look back in the mirror, wondering at the pearls and diamonds that are expertly knotted into the white gold, before pulls it up into the twisted horn in its center. At its crest is a large ruby. The Shadowcavern dwarves, experts in mining, had likely provided it to King Dario at his request.

Not too many other people know it is supposed to be a red diamond, and that it had been lost along with the princess.

"You look beautiful," Juni whispers as she steps back from me. "You're doing Princess Cari proud, God give her soul peace."

"You don't think she's dead, do you?"

"Honestly? I don't know what to think." She sighs. "So I pray. I hope. But I don't know. I can only trust." Her wrinkled hands clasp together, and I can see she is upset. She likely didn't mean to comment so darkly on the princess' fate.

"I try to do the same," I say, and at my confession, she relaxes.

"I pray for you, too," Juni admits, patting my head affectionately. "Once Ari is gone, we will have no heir to the Unicorn's blessing, and all the realms will be in danger of falling apart."

She looks out the window of my room, and I follow her gaze. The sky is full of rainbows as the evening draws near.

Juni is right, but she is also wrong. The king has already been facing opposition, as there are growing factions within the kingdom that oppose his rule. If they were to find out that the Unicorn's blessing is no longer on the Queen's household, it will be the end of Toulacoeur.

And the end of my life, too.

After Cari was kidnapped, Kleon vowed only to come back when she returned. The queen has suffered in sickness since then, both at the loss of her daughter and the rejection of her unicorn protector.

Princess Cari is now the only one who is able to summon Kleon to the kingdom, and since I am not really her, no matter how much I may look like her, I will be branded a traitor to the people of the Honeyspice Lands and their leader, the Alpha Kitsune.

It is my duty, as a slave to the king and queen, not to let the kingdom know the truth about Cari's fate; they might eventually find out the truth, but the sooner they do, the sooner I die, executed as a traitor.

Trying not to think of my worst possible fate, I follow Juni out of my room down to join the procession.

The sun has fully set now, and the rainbows of the skies are now bathed in moonlight.

Kiro is standing behind his parents, holding the reins of two horses. One is for me, and the other is for him. I will be riding next to him as we visit the capital, before we return to the courtyard gardens for Kiro's birthday ball.

I straighten as I walk gallantly down to meet them. I know I am not truly worthy of their love and affection, but I want to be.

C. S. JOHNSON

Thank you for reading! Please leave a review for this book and check out www.csjohnson.me for other books and updates!

C. S. JOHNSON

www.ingramcontent.com/pod-product-compliance
Lightning Source LLC
Chambersburg PA
CBHW070030300426
43673CB00103B/87